MW01175136

Praise for Mark Brady's *Right Listening* ...

"This delightful little book contains huge treasures, the ones that can bring us back into the joy of being human together. I imagine that if a reader only focused on two or three of the many skills given here, that they would quickly become skilled in listening, and would fall in love with the places that real conversation always takes us."   ~ Margaret J. Wheatley, PhD

author, *Turning to One Another* and *Leadership and the New Science*

"*Right Listening* is a delight. It is simple, direct and profound; easy to read and follow. People crave attention and understanding and this book will help those in all relationships improve their ability to connect, listen and love."   ~ Frederic Luskin, PhD
Forgive for Good
Director, Stanford Forgiveness Project

"A true treasure! When we shift our attention toward listening, our whole world changes. Learning to listen is equal to learning to love. This creative handbook teaches us that learning to listen does not have to be a mystery. Rather, there are tangible ways that we can deepen our capacity for empathy and presence - transforming our relationships with others and ourselves. It has helped me to be a better educator, spouse, and parent. *Right Listening* is a rare gift indeed!"

~ Ruth Cox, PhD
Institute for Holistic Healing Studies
San Francisco State University

"Listening is no small skill, and so this little book is no small matter. Everyone who wants better relationships and more productivity should read this. It's fun, easy to read and speaks to the heart of the matter. I think it's a winner."

~ Richard Carlson, PhD
Don't Sweat the Small Stuff

"The foundation of good teaching is the ability to listen. Although the authors write for a much broader audience, they have provided an indispensable tool – actually, a great gift – for classroom instructors. I will carry **Right Listening** in my pocket on a daily basis."

~ Mary Fainsod Katzenstein, PhD
Government Department
Cornell University

"When you do what I do for a living, it's rare to find a resource that's practical, satisfying, learnable and inspirational all in the same breath. *Right Listening* is all that and much, much more. Two copies should be issued simultaneously with every marriage license."

~ Peter Pearson, PhD
In Quest of the Mythical Mate
co-founder, The Couples Institute

"Reading **Right Listening** should be required for all human beings, as soon as they can read and as long as their eyesight allows."

~ Joan C. King, PhD
and author of **Cellular Wisdom**

"This book may be little, but the significance of its message is big…very big. With appealing modesty and great sensitivity, Mark Brady offers the reader a wealth of practical tips for how to listen more attentively and effectively to others. If only a fraction of this wise advice could be put into practice, the benefits – for listener and speaker alike – would be enormous."

~ Doug McAdam, PhD, father and
former director, Stanford Center
for Advanced Study in the Behavioral Sciences
Dynamics of Contention

For Muriel

A Father's Book of Listening

Essential practices
for truly loving our children

by

Mark Brady, Ph.D.

Paideia* Press
Langley, WA

Paideia Press
P.O. Box 1294
Langley, WA 98260 (206) 201-2212
paideia@gmail.com

*PAIDEIA (pie-day-a) from the Greek pais, paidos:
    lifelong learning that pays special attention
    to the spirit, heart or essence of things.

Library of Congress Cataloging-in-Publication Data

Brady, Mark, PhD
A Father's Book of Listening / Mark Brady
    p. cm.

ISBN-10 1-5029622-2-5
ISBN-13   978-1-5029622-2-5

153.7'7–dc27

                                    2015111946

19 18 17 16 15
 6 5 4   3 2

Cover designed by Roosje Penfold,
Mind That Bird Design
www.mindthatbird.us
Set in Times New Roman and Franklin Gothic Medium
Printed in the United States of America

WHEN SOMEONE DEEPLY LISTENS TO YOU

When someone deeply listens to you
it is like holding out a dented cup
you've had since childhood
and watching it fill up with
cold, fresh water.
When it balances on top of the brim,
you are understood.
When it overflows and touches your skin,
you are loved.

When someone deeply listens to you
the room where you stay
starts a new life
and the place where you wrote
your first poem
begins to glow in your mind's eye.
It is as if gold has been discovered!

When someone deeply listens to you
your bare feet are on the earth
and a beloved land that seemed distant
is now at home within you.

~ John Fox

How to get the most out of this book

The feedback I've gotten from readers of early editions of *A Father's Book of Listening* indicates that the practices in this little book truly are life-changing and love-affirming . . . *if* they are read repeatedly and practiced often. I suggest you first read the titles and mark those that resonate with you. Scan the titles of the various skills and start with one that you are most curious about. Read it and begin to put it into action. Then read another and do the same. Keep this book on your nightstand, or in the bathroom and read a new skill or refresh an old one regularly. Many readers report they keep a copy of the book at the ready – in the visor of their car, or on their desk at work for handy reference. For many of us, learning to listen deeply is like learning a whole new foreign language. Feel free to write in the book. Be creative in doing whatever you need to do in order to get the most out of the practices.

Another way to get the most out of *A Father's Book of Listening* is to create a community of practice. Ask friends, colleagues, or members of your spiritual community to practice with you. Small, faith-based groups have been effective in helping each other learn to listen most skillfully. If you feel stress, sorrow, anger or any other strong emotion while reading a particular skill, listen carefully to this body-message. Don't force a practice that is overly charged for you. Take your time. Be curious. Play. Have fun while you learn one of the most powerful parenting skills available to you as a father – the art of skillful listening.

Table of Contents

Introduction

"Listen and understand me."　　　　　*Page 37*

14. Regularly practice kenosis
15. Listen for feelings
16. Never, never, never scream at your kids
17. NEVER, NEVER, NEVER scream at your kids
18. Avoid letting your story take over their story
19. Repair relationship ruptures as soon as possible
20. Learn and practice contingent communication
21.   Be genuinely curious
22. Listen for underlying needs
23. Identify defensiveness; practice non-defensiveness
24. Listen for differences
25. Relax and laugh
26. Develop "second attention at the edge"

Section Two Reflection Questions　　　*Page 52*

Introduction

The healing power of being listened to has been recognized for centuries. Many of us fathers know the powerful experience of being listened to by a skillful listener – a mentor, "rabbi" or coach who makes us feel deeply heard, appreciated, accepted, understood. Being listened to enlivens us and inspires opportunities to explore what we think, how we feel, what we want, who we are, and who we're becoming. It's absolutely the same for our children.

In this little book you'll discover the many benefits available to children and to fathers who become skilled listeners, benefits that are often hidden and overlooked.

Listening grows neural connections in our brains and feeds our hearts. Throughout the lifespan it increases connections in the "gray matter" and "white matter" in the brain. Those connections can help us create better relationships with our children and ourselves. Skilled Listening Fathers experience more joy, peace and ease with their kids, and they acquire useful communication tools and new perspectives to meet life's challenges.

After reading the first printing of this little book, many fathers thanked me for the skills they learned from these pages. They told me how powerful the listening practices have been in helping to connect deeply not only with their children, but with partners, friends, business colleagues and themselves.

The world needs more fathers who are skilled listeners, but moreover, it needs the attentive, opened hearts of those fathers who model sincerity, concern and compassion for others to their kids. It needs the questions that men who are Skilled Listening Fathers ask themselves. And children need to hear the questions such fathers can ask them, such as, "What's working you today?" "What's troubling you?" and "How can I help?" Skilled Listening Fathers invite their children to speak truthfully and they hold the things they hear sacred. Such fathers do not necessarily try to change things, fix them, or turn away from them. Here in this little book are some tools we need to become such fathers, to learn to listen deeply to ourselves and to our children.

May we be blessed and surrounded by children who love and trust us enough to show and tell us who they really are.

Mark Brady
Whidbey Island, WA
January, 2015

"Being listened to is so close to being loved that most people don't know the difference."

~ David Augsburger

"I just need you to listen to me."

A young black South African woman taught some of my friends a profound lesson about listening. She was sitting in a circle of women from many nations and each woman had the chance to tell a story from her life. When her turn came, she began quietly to tell a story of true horror – of how she had found her grandparents slaughtered in their village. Many of the women were Westerners, and in the presence of such pain, they instinctively wanted to do something. They wanted to fix it, to make it better, anything to remove the pain of this tragedy from such a young life. The young woman felt their compassion, but also felt them closing in. She put her hands up, as if to push back their desire to help. She said, "I don't need you to fix me. I just need you to listen to me."

She taught many women that day that being listened to is enough. If we can speak our story and know that others truly hear it, we are somehow healed by that. During the Truth and Reconciliation Commission hearings in South Africa, many who testified to the atrocities they had endured would speak of being healed by their own testimony. They knew that many people were listening to their story. One young man who had been blinded when a policeman shot him in the face at close range said, "I feel what has brought my eyesight back is to come here and tell the story. I feel what has been making me sick all this time is the fact that I couldn't tell my story. But now it feels like I've got my sight back by coming here and telling you the story."

~ Margaret Wheatley

1. Talk less, listen more

This is the simplest and fastest change we can make to become more skillful as a Listening Father. In conversations with our kids, we can hear who's doing most of the talking. If it's our children, that's a good start. From there, we can employ additional skills that can further improve our listening.

However, if *we* are talking most of the time – which is quite common, since fathers are teachers, too – there are practices we can do to shift the balance toward listening more. The first thing is simply to notice when we're talking and not listening. Without this primary awareness, little else can happen. *With* this awareness, a number of options become possible. First of all, we now have the choice to decide to stop talking. There are many ways to accomplish this. We can ask questions such as, "What's on your mind?" "What do you think?" and "Tell me more."

There are additional means and methods for passing conversations over to our kids as well. Smiling or nodding often encourages them to talk. A simple statement like, "I have been doing most of the talking; I'll stop now and listen," is a direct invitation for kids to talk. The possibilities for gracefully shifting from speaking to listening are limitless. Make up any that you feel comfortable with and practice using them.

Becoming a Listening Father starts first with the intention. The desire to talk less and listen more is a powerful step in loving our kids and ourselves. In a world full of talkers, a Skillful Listening Father shines like the Hope Diamond.

Practice: *Identify a time with your kids when you do most of the talking. Utilize one skill from this book to swing the balance toward them talking more. What's the experience like?*

2. Don't interrupt unnecessarily

Many times as we're listening to our children, the things they say will emotionally trigger us. Their words may provoke anger, sadness, fear or some other strong feeling in us. Such feelings can generate an uncontrollable impulse to override what our kids are saying in order to relieve our own anxiety. This is another one of those impulses – like not letting your story take over another's (Skill No. 18) – which is import-ant to learn to limit in order to be a more skillful listener.

When we cut kids off in mid-sentence or interrupt by finishing their thoughts out loud for them, we're being disrespectful, and we could be harming our health! Dr. Paul Pearsall, the author of *The Last Self-Help Book You'll Ever Need* writes, "Stop expressing, representing, and asserting yourself. Shut up and listen. Research shows that people who interrupt are three times more likely to die of a heart attack than those who don't, and that (relationships) usually fail because of too much communication, not too little."

When we interrupt them, the message we send to our kids is "What I have to say is more important than what you have to say. It's so important that I won't shut up and let you finish." By learning to regularly hold our tongues in daily interactions with our kids, and becoming genuinely curious about what they are saying, we greatly improve our listening skills and also our own health.

Practice: *Pay attention to how frequently you and other people interrupt one another in everyday discussions. Take steps to reduce your own pattern of interrupting your kids. Notice the positive effect it has on the way they relate to you. For example, one helpful practice might be to place your tongue against the roof of your mouth and hold it there.*

3. Create an atmosphere of trust

Communication that most powerfully connects us with our children occurs when trust exists. Fathers who are skillful listeners works intentionally to build trust. This means not putting our kids on guard, and having a genuine, expressed concern for their psychological safety and well-being.

There are many ways to begin to establish trust. Most effective is to be genuinely trustworthy. Trustworthy people rarely betray trust. When your central concern is for the safety and well-being of yourself and others, often there's nothing special that needs to be done. Many kids intuitively sense this authentic orientation.

Although we like to think we are trustworthy, some-times old patterns of behavior, shaped by early life events (see pages 93-95), can cause us to allow unconscious needs, wants and desires to prevent us from fully concerning ourselves with the care and safety of others. Such early life events can keep us from taking care of ourselves as well. Learning what early life events may be getting in the way of listening skillfully to our kids, as well as being able to create an environment of trust, is vitally important to every father. If genuine trust is to be established, such impacts from early life events need to be compassionately brought into the light of day and resolved.

Practice: *Are you the person your kids feel safe enough to tell their deepest truths to? What are the elements that contribute most positively to that feeling? What's one thing you can do to move more in the direction of being someone your kids implicitly trust?*

4. Listen for disrespect

Think of your last conflict or disagreement you had with your kids. You may not be able to clearly recall exactly what it was about, but very likely you can recall how you felt. That's because the seeming cause of many conflicts – the unkept promise, the misunderstood action or a truth untold – is not really what's at the heart of the matter.

Whenever conflict arises, one of two things is often taking place. (We'll discuss the second one in the next practice.) In daily life many fathers know they feel upset, or angry, but they fail to realize deep down they're feeling disrespected. Disrespect is a tricky emotion. A father or child can feel disrespected even though neither might feel they are being disrespectful. What is a father to do if disrespect can be so easily triggered, but not easily identified?

Fortunately, there are telltale signs if someone feels disrespected. Some common signs are expressions of anger or sarcasm, verbal attacks, hostile body language, or refusing to communicate – the silent treatment. A Skillful Listening Father inquires about these observations and considers that disrespect might be at issue. Permitting oneself time to think about things, helps allow room for feelings of disrespect to be identified. Once they have been identified, a father can move toward a solution or make any amends that may be necessary.

Practice: *Listen for the clues in the next conflict with your kids that indicates you or they may be feeling disrespected. Once the real issue – evoked feelings of disrespect – is resolved, coming to agreement and resolving disagreements involving secondary concerns becomes much more workable.*

5. Listen for mutual purpose

The second cause of many conflicts between fathers and their children is a lack or loss of mutual purpose. Until mutual purposes can be identified or reaffirmed, very few such conflicts will ever be easily resolved.

Even the most bitter of enemies, by simple virtue of their common humanity, have mutual purposes in common, i.e. survival needs, self-esteem needs and the need for respect. What fathers and children are often in conflict over, are the best ways to get such needs met.

However, if respect can be a safe ground, then a foundation will exist for exploring and/or re-establishing mutual purpose. Differences may still exist, but the possibility for coming to agreement is significantly enhanced if mutual respect and common purpose are identified and set solidly in place.

Fathers can listen for mutual purpose then, by first hearing all the ways they are working at cross-purposes with their kids. Next they can listen for the places where mutual purpose might be hiding in the conflict. This doesn't mean that resolving conflict is easy and won't require hard work, but by focusing on mutual respect and mutual purpose, a Listening Father will be addressing the things that can constructively make conflict resolution a possibility.

Practice: *The next time you find yourself in a conflict with your children, look for where any cross purposes may exist. Then look for where a discussion of mutual purposes might begin.*

6. *Be slow to disagree, argue or criticize*

Sometimes the conversations we have with our kids are laced with criticism, argument and disagreement. When we engage in these behaviors as a father, we can't really hear what our kids are trying to say. We are attempting to get our point across and are not open to hearing what they are actually trying to express. A Listening Father listens to kids beliefs, points of view and truthful versions of their experiences. It may be hard to hear things we don't like (Skill No. 35), things we want them to change or stop doing, but skillful listening allows a child full rein to say whatever they need to say.

Using other listening skills recommended in this book can help put an end to argument, criticism and disagreement. It takes discernment and practice to be open to things that are difficult to hear or what we think our kids need to correct, but in the long run, bottom-line truths that have the room to be fully expressed by our kids is worth far more than "being right," or "changing their mind." Being slow to disagree, argue or criticize goes a long way to allow truth, understanding and compassion to possibly unfold.

Practice: *Observe several different conversations with your kids over the next few days. Listen for how much argument, disagreement, or criticism passes for conversation. Pay particular attention to its effect on your child.*

7. Pay attention to the need for conversation control

How many times have you observed or taken part in a conversation where you and your kids are talking at the same time? If such a situation goes on for any duration, each of you will most likely keep raising his or her voice, trying to out-decibel the other until it actually becomes quite comical.

In such situations very little listening is occurring, and a power struggle is taking place, even though that might not be so obvious. In fact, many exchanges that pass as dialogues are really exercises in domination and competition for conversational control. The irony is, in many conversations it is the *listener* who holds the greatest power and control by virtue of what he or she chooses to ignore or respond to. By electing to selectively attend to content and perhaps focus on emotional tone or immediate context, a Skillful Listening Father can turn a conversation or conflict 180 degrees in a matter of moments.

Many parents are reluctant to give over control in a discussion for fear that it is something given over forever or that it signifies weakness. The biblical injunction to "seek first to understand, and then to be understood" is good advice. It's not only possible, but advantageous to regularly give the floor over to our kids. Once a child has had the opportunity to express what they need to, frequently they have more energy available to pay attention to what you have to say. As it is written in an ancient book of wisdom: "Yield and overcome."

Practice: *Observe conversations with your kids over the course of several days. Who does most of the talking? Who interrupts? Can you see where the balance of control lies? Are you aware of control issues in your own conversations with others? With whom and over what?*

8. Cultivate "Beginner's Ear"

Beginner's Ear is a way of paying attention to the present moment that is open and curious. It holds a sense of wonder and delight and the possibility of discovery in the midst of focusing on increasingly finer detail.

To gain a sense of what Beginner's Ear might be like, we can think of how the sounds of the world affected us as a small child. We can recall what it was like on a warm summer night and we heard that very first cricket chirp and then heard smaller details – the rhythm, the silence between chirps, and the answering call of the other crickets.

Sounds of childhood might be hearing can also help us recall the feel and flavor of Beginner's Ear. Everything is new and thrilling because we are curious and can pay close attention. It is paying close attention to ever-finer detail that lies at the heart of Beginner's Ear. Attention to discriminating detail is the remedy that literally works best to keep things from "going in one ear and out the other."

Practice: *Hold a conversation with your child and listen with a new sense of curiosity and wonder. What are some things you hear that you may not have heard before?*

9. Get comfortable with silence

The plain and simple truth is that few of us – parents or professionals – are perfectly comfortable with silence. We live and work with radios and TVs blaring. We use cell phones and carry on conversations in spaces that used to be silent and sacred. The extinction of silence is taking place all over the world, right before our very ears.

Becoming comfortable with silence is a necessary and critical for fathers who want to become skillful listeners. It is in the silent spaces between parents and children that the Creative Wild can begin to emerge. In silence, something bordering on magic transpires: as a Listening Father we can offer our kids a chance to discover what they think, how they feel, what they want.

In silence, we can listen to our children and ourselves and discover what's required to live more fully. MIT professor, Peter Senge identifies this as "generative listening" – the art of developing deeper silences that work to slow the mind's hearing to the ear's and life's natural speed.

One way to become increasingly comfortable with silence is to spend increasing amounts of time with our kids in it. As we do, silence's rhythms and sensations will become intimately familiar to us. It is, after all, this spacious emptiness at the sub-atomic level that quantum physicists tell us mostly makes up who we are !

Practice: *Make it a point to be aware of how silence around your kids feels to you. Does it cause anxiety? Do you automatically rush to fill the space? Do they? Be mindful of the quiet and see if you can allow silence to be a part of every day.*

10. Manage emotional reactivity

Nothing stops our children from saying what they really want to say faster than unbridled emotional reactivity. Speaking in loud, angry tones, replying with sarcasm, personal attacks, or even silent fuming all work to stifle authentic self-expression. Emotional reactivity not only interferes with listening, it can seriously damage our relationship with our kids. It undermines trust and is disrespectful. Unchecked emotional reactivity is irresponsible, since the inability to control or regulate your internal emotional state is yours.

Fathers who frequently communicate in this reactive manner say, "That's just the way I am. Don't take it personally." Such justification demonstrates little real understanding of reactivity's powerful negative impact on the communication process. Lack of awareness doesn't mean that the negative impact is not happening just the same.

At the root of all reactivity is a behavior pattern often based upon old wounds from times when we've felt belittled, humiliated, misunderstood or disrespected ourselves (See pages 93-95). Making peace with and healing these old wounds is Job Number One for a Listening Father. Some parents will argue, "I don't have control over what I say. Things just pop out of my mouth." The work of a Skillful Listening Father is to learn how to act in *response* to the thoughts that fuel the emotional reactivity behind the thoughts, and not simply react instinctively.

Practice: *Spend some time during the coming week noticing the power that the things your kids say has to move you reactively. Notice what triggers you. What needs of yours might be going unfulfilled? Can you find or think of a positive way to get such needs met?*

11. Avoid "shoulding" on children

Perhaps we often find ourselves offering our kids unsolicited advice. As well-meaning as we may be, unless older kids specifically ask for it, advice doesn't work. It's rarely heeded and seldom needed. Living inside each of us is a wealth of wisdom and experience that is much more reliable, insight-ful and trustworthy than advice offered by parents. Telling kids what they "should" do, at best, runs interference, blocking access to this internal wisdom. At worst, "shoulding" on our kids ends up being judgmental and disrespectful. It also leaves us saddled with the responsibility to fix their problems. Isn't it better to help them find their own fixes?

When we find ourselves tempted to tell our kids what they "should" do, it might be better to reflect back and ask Strategic Questions in an attempt to put them in touch with their own inner needs (Skill No. 44). "What does your gut tell you?" "If you're of two minds, what is each telling you?" "What outcome would be optimal in this situation?" Continually inviting our kids to look to themselves, to take initiative and set intentions, will go a long way toward making everyone's life easier.

Practice: *For the next week, pay attention to the ways you are tempted to give advice to your kids. Practice skillful ways of returning the responsibility for solving their problems back onto them.*

12. Don't father by the book, father by the child

Each year several dozen parenting books are published in the United States. Much of what was "true" when Doctor Spock first wrote his best-selling, *Baby and Child Care,*[2] has been rewritten in the intervening years. Field research and advances in technology that allow for more precise observation and assessment, force us to revise what we know and think about parenting.

So, with parenting information under constant revision and flux, what's a father to do? If reading and research is something you enjoy and get benefit from, by all means continue to do it. Just don't use what you learn in a haphazard, rigid manner. Better is to pay attention to, and take our cues directly from our children them-selves. Young children know what they need, and because they don't have good language skills, they develop "creative" ways to let parents know about those needs. Much of what constitutes effective parenting is like detective work, learning to discern and translate a child's needs in ways that contribute optimally to their maturation and development.

Practice: *What are some of the unique ways your children let you know they have needs that are not being met? Things like bedwetting or having "accidents" can be examples. So can forgetting things or writing with crayons on the living room wall. Assume that such behavior is expressing unmet needs and see if you can watch and listen to find out what those needs might be.*

13. Establish support for speaking truth to power

It is often difficult for kids to speak truthfully to people who hold power over then – like teachers and parents. Listening Fathers know this and take it to heart when listening to their kids. They encourage their children to feel empowered to say what's true with no fear of reprisal. A Listening Father can listen with compassion, hear a child's tender truth and hold it gently, no matter how distressing it may be. The Lakota warrior and wise man, Crazy Horse once warned, "Power must listen with honest ears to the whispers of the powerless." To become a father with honest ears – someone to whom children can speak the truth – you must be kind. You must know that your power makes it difficult for kids to speak openly and truthfully unless you deliberately do things to make it happen.

One obvious guideline for fathers is to refrain at all times from ridiculing, blaming, shaming, or condemning our kids. By doing so we begin to establish ourselves as fathers who welcome the truth no matter how disturbing or how poorly expressed it might be. Thus, we build a flawless reputation for welcoming and cherishing our children as truth-tellers.

Practice: *Notice over the next week, any time you have the impulse to tell a lie, either by commission or omission. What is the fear that underlies it? What might work to permit you to tell the truth to the other person? Then, notice how your children speak to you. Can you tell when they might be telling you what they think you want to hear, rather than the whole truth and nothing but the truth?*

Section One Reflection Questions

Of these first 13 skills, which stand out the most as you practice to become a Skillful Listening Father?

What have you heard that you haven't been able to hear before you began practicing these skills?

Complete this sentence: "I am working most to create an atmosphere of trust by..."

Notes to yourself...

"We do not believe in ourselves until someone
reveals that something deep inside us
is valuable, worth listening to,
worthy of our trust,
sacred to our touch."

~ *e. e. cummings*

"Listen and understand me."

When I ask you to listen and you start giving advice, you have not done what I have asked. When I ask you to listen and you start telling me why I shouldn't feel the way I do, you are invalidating my feelings. When I ask you to listen and you start trying to solve my problems, I feel underestimated and disempowered. When I ask you to listen and you start telling me what I need to do I feel offended, pressured and controlled. When I ask you to listen, it does not mean I am helpless. I may be faltering, depressed or discouraged, but I am not helpless. When I ask you to listen and you do things which I can and need to do for myself, you hurt my self-esteem. But when you accept the way I feel, then I don't need to spend time and energy trying to defend myself or convince you, and I can focus on figuring out why I feel the way I feel and what to do about it. And when I do that, I don't need advice, just support, trust and encouragement. Please remember that what you think are irrational feelings always makes sense if you take the time to listen and understand me.

~ An adolescent's plea to adults

14. Regularly practice kenosis

Listening is more than simply taking in the words our children and others say. It often includes a requirement for us to empty our hearts and minds of personal agendas in order to connect directly with them. There's a wonderful Greek word that perfectly describes this process: *kenosis.*

Kenosis is derived from *kengo,* which has several related meanings. The primary meaning for skilled listening is "to empty oneself." It is an empty, open state that allows for high levels of listening.

M. Scott Peck, noted author of *The Road Less Traveled* says, "… the setting aside of one's own prejudices, frames of reference and desires so as to experience as far as possible the speaker's world from the inside, steps inside his or her shoes. This unification of speaker and listener is actually an extension and enlargement of ourselves, and new knowledge is always gained from this. Moreover, since true listening involves a setting aside of the self, it also temporarily involves a total acceptance of the other. Sensing this acceptance, the speaker will feel less and less vulnerable, and more and more inclined to open up the inner recesses of his or her mind to the listener. As this happens, speaker and listener begin to appreciate each other more and more, and the dance of love is begun again." Can you imagine a more wonderful example between a father and his children of kenosis in action?

Practice: *Deliberately listen to your kids without any particular agenda. Free yourself from your own world and* *focus on them. Put aside your physical, mental, or emotional needs and aches and pains and focus solely on their words. Empty yourself of all thoughts of you and what you think reality and truth are.*

15. Listen for feelings

When listening to content of what our kids say, it is often the emotion that underlies their words that will be most significant. Emotion is what we hear deeply and respond to most strongly, often without even realizing it. Feelings guide us as speakers and listeners to deeper truths.

Before we can recognize and authentically respond to our children's feelings, however, we are well-served to learn to recognize and become comfortable with our own. For some fathers, this work is like attempting to learn a foreign language, and a difficult one at that.

When we are comfortable knowing what we feel, we will be able to listen better for the emotional content of what our children say and feel. When we listen for feelings, we begin to hear things not just with our ears, but with our heart and gut as well. It is what our kids feel that they want us to know and understand, even if they can't clearly verbalize it with their limited vocabulary.

Practice: *How do you know what you feel when you feel it? Spend some time identifying one of the five major feelings: mad, sad, glad, excited, or scared. Notice the place in your body that you predominately experience each feeling. This is a powerful form of self-listening. Then listen for a child's emotional content. Close your* *eyes and open your heart to what is really being presented.*

16. Never, never, never scream at your kids

Ralph Waldo Emerson suggested that sometimes a scream is better than a thesis, but rarely is that true when it comes to parenting. If you're a parent who attempts to control, reprimand, discipline or get your kids' attention by scream- ing at them, psychologist Sarah Radcliffe suggests this is a negative parenting pattern that you don't want to continue. Whether you know it or not, whether you believe it or not, research shows that screaming parents cause their children considerable harm. A study in a 2001 Journal of American Psychiatry agrees: emotional abuse was more predictive of mental illness than either physical or sexual abuse!

So, what might you do in place of screaming? Many things. To get their attention, you can say a child's name repeatedly and firmly until they make eye contact. Then make whatever specific requests you wish. To discipline children, or to get them to perform chores or homework, or come to dinner, call them once. After that, go to where they are and, without anger, gently take them by the hand and wordlessly lead them to where you want them to be, and tell them again what you want.

Practice: *The next time you find yourself screaming at your kids, STOP! Be aware that you are causing them great harm. Find some way to get your message across as if your children are people that you really, really love.*

17. NEVER, NEVER, NEVER SCREAM AT YOUR KIDS

Screaming at children significantly impairs their brain development. Dr. Allan Shore, at the UCLA Neuro-psychiatric Institute, explains that a number of times, all through development, children's brains undergo massive pruning – as much as 50% of the brain's 86 billion neurons.[11] And which brain structures ultimately receive the bulk of that pruning has great impact on development.

If you scream at your children, you repeatedly activate structures in the limbic system like the amygdala and the hippocampus – structures that regulate "flight or fight" reactions. Repeated activation tells the brain that the environment is not safe, thus a maximum amount of interconnecting neurons in these areas must remain intact.

Because pruning has to happen, neurons will be pruned from structures like the frontal cortex where higher-order functions tend to be regulated. Thus, screaming at your kids works to impair their intellectual and emotional development by forcing the brain to retain neurons in the limbic area where they are most needed. Commit to finding alternative ways that do not cause this kind of damage.

Practice: *Make it a practice to find ways to let your children know that you are a safe person to be with, and that everything in their daily environment and experience contributes to their safety. When they are old enough, actively include children in decision-making processes, especially with things that affect them directly.*

18. Avoid letting your story take over their story

Often, when we listen to our children and other people, what they say strikes a responsive chord in us. We may have had similar thoughts or experiences. In an attempt to empathize and connect with them, we may feel the urge to tell our own related stories. Resist this impulse. It doesn't work.

When we tell our own story, we shift the focus away from our kids, perhaps for extended periods. Inevitably, this leaves them feeling cut off, frustrated and disrespected. When this happens, more often than not, our children will stop talking and perhaps feel resentful or disrespected.

Perhaps the story that you have interrupted is only the beginning of something a child is trying to explore and find their way more deeply into, or perhaps it is something they simply need to get off their chest. To short-circuit this process with our own story is in a subtle way saying that what you have to say is more important than what they have to say. We all know how badly that feels.

Practice: *Next time you find yourself telling your story in response to someone else's, stop and apologize for interrupting. Ask the child or person to please continue. To help get them back on track, ask a question about their story and begin listening anew.*

19. *Repair relationship ruptures as soon as possible*

Screaming at our children, hitting them, sending them to their room for extended periods, ignoring them, putting them down, disrespecting them – all these actions rupture the parent-child relationship. Frequent, unrepaired ruptures that go on unaddressed, damage a child's vulnerable, developing brain. Such unrepaired ruptures can lead our children to withdraw or to react aggressively. As parents, one primary responsibility is to reflect on how our own actions may be contributing to our children's unwanted behavior.

As soon as things have calmed down, relationship repair work must begin. Successful repair work cannot be made from an angry or resentful emotional state. Successful rupture repair often begins with the parent admitting to, and taking responsibility for their own out-of-control behavior. Usually such behavior has fear or high levels of stress or anxiety at its roots. From there, one useful response is to make ourselves available for what our kids might have to say, blocking nothing (See Skill No. 25).

Practice: *Think of several instances where you have felt overly reactive to things your child said or did. What fears or anxieties might lie at the root of your reactivity? Are there still raw feelings involved? Read over this practice and being this important repair work as soon as possible.*

20. Learn and practice contingent communication

Contingent or collaborative communication between people works to positively increase neural connectivity in both brains. There are three conditions that must be met for a communication to be *truly* contingent:

1. the parent must accurately receive the words or nonverbal signals a child is sending;

2. the parent must be able to accurately process and understand the signals;

3. and most importantly, a parent must respond in a timely and effective manner. A timely and effective response signals to a message-sending brain that the people around them understand them. It makes children feel seen and safe. Who our children become is in large part a result of how important people respond to them.

Contingent communication works to help organize the brain, and at the same time it teaches children and adults how to work together, how to collaborate with each other and with other people.

Practice: *Consider all the different channels through which your children might send you messages, for example: eye contact, facial expressions, voice tone, gestures, along with timing and intensity of their responses. What might be some positive ways of receiving and answering messages that might be different than how you might typically respond?*

21. Be genuinely curious

Some fathers just seem to have a natural inclination towards curiosity. They ask a lot of questions and explore new things with gusto. These fathers are more prone to be curious about others and naturally want to listen and know more about them. Rob Brown, a California public relations executive, has a way of making everyone he talks to feel extremely important. He asks question after question, sincerely wanting to know: "And then what happened?" or "And how did you feel?" His favorite response to a speaker is, "Tell me more."

For those of us not born with a strong inclination to curiousness, we can develop it by remembering what it was like when we were a young child and everything was new and fascinating. When we try on the eyes and ears of our children to encounter our world and the people in it, we become more curious about who they are and what they might want us to know.

Curiosity makes us sincerely interested in our children and who they are becoming. When we are curious, we ask more open-ended questions and are eager for the answers. Our curiosity conveys to a child that we care for and appreciate them. Curiosity fuels a desire to lead our children ever more deeply into their truth and invites them to share it with us.

Practice: *Put on "the eyes and ears of a child" the next time you speak to them. What things do you become curious about? What questions can you ask to discover more about that child?*

22. Listen for underlying needs

In one way or another, most every communication from our kids is an expression of a need. It may take the direct form of a straightforward statement: "I'm hungry," "I'm bored," or "I hate school."

Communication can also indirectly express needs that lie below the surface: "I'm hungry" may mean, "I'm needing emotional nourishment." "I'm bored" may mean, "I'm looking for human contact and connection." "I hate school" may mean "There's a bully at school who scares me." A Skillful Listening Father listens for the underlying needs of his kids. To get to underlying needs, we can ask a simple question – "Why is that?" or "What do you need exactly?"

Listening for needs works to identify areas of common interest around which positive, creative interactions can be built. For example, if we listen for the message underlying "I'm bored," we can open up a host of possibilities for change. But it all starts with the realization that virtually all communication is intended to express a multiplicity of needs. The Listening Father is constantly listening for what those needs may be. Ralph Nichols, America's Dean of Listening Research, summed it up best when he said, "The most basic of all human needs is the need to understand and be understood. The best way to understand (our children) is to listen to them."

Practice: *Things that our children might need from any communication often are hidden, even from them. Over the next few days, spend some time asking them this simple question: "What is it you need?" Simply asking doesn't* *make you required to provide what they need, but it does help both of you to know.*

23. Identify defensiveness; practice non-defensiveness

When our kids feel under attack, either rightfully or wrongfully, they will frequently defend themselves with either silence or "violence."

When they react with silence, all conversation stops. When they react with violence, it's often by retaliatory verbal attacks or physical acting-out – slamming doors or kicking or throwing things. This can escalate to further violence.

Violence can take more subtle forms as well. Sarcastic or snide remarks like, "Who died and made you king?" or "Why don't you show us the right way to do it then, Mr. Big Shot?" also have the seeds of violence in them. Any remark that has the effect of diminishing, discounting, belittling, or marginalizing children has violence at its core.

We need to recognize that a defensive response is often activated by either our own behavior or our own verbal responses. It is a practice to learn not to defend against the things that have caused our kids to react with silence or violence, but rather we can help them search for what *we* may be doing to cause them to feel attacked. Skillful listening can mend relationship ruptures, thus Listening Fathers are open to inviting their children to talk about things further – to "use words, not war." Defensiveness begets more conflict. Listening Fathers listen for defensiveness and the reasons for it, and offer apologies for their part and make amends when necessary.

57

Practice: *Pay attention when kids begin to defend themselves in a discussion. What might you have said or done that triggered the reaction? Do you easily recognize when you or your child feels the need to defend?*

24. Listen for differences

When we listen to our kids, often what we listen for are the things we understand or things we agree with. We find comfort in discovering the ways that they are like us. When our kids say things or act differently than us it makes us uncomfortable. When they actually turn out to be *very* different from us, it can make us extremely uncomfortable. We don't necessarily like to see or hear about differences.

A Listening Father deliberately seeks out and pays attention to the ways our kids are different from us. We begin to appreciate the ways they have been shaped, molded, and often distorted by culture, schooling, family of origin, genetic makeup, and any number of other unknown factors. Like snowflakes, no two children out of billions and billions are ever exactly alike.

After we've learned to listen for differences and to develop an appreciation for them in our kids, we can cherish and celebrate their special uniqueness. With this perspective we can deeply appreciate the power and beauty in complexity and diversity.

Practice: *Spend time paying close attention to things your children do and say that surprise you, or that you don't* *understand, or that you disagree with. Consider what you expected them to say. What assumptions underlie your expectations? Can you appreciate how their differences hold the potential to make their world an exciting and interesting place?*

25. Relax and laugh

Learning something new takes time and effort. It's easy to get too caught up in the learning. When that happens, we need to lift our heads up, look around, relax and pay attention to other things in our lives. We can temporarily make parent-ing a part-time job.

There is much to laugh about in learning to skillfully listen to our kids. Miscommunication is the norm. Sometimes, it's a wonder we're able to understand one another at all, especially when we consider that of the 800 English words that most of us use on a daily basis, each has an average of 17 different meanings! (Other languages the world over, have similar complexities). Add to that the fact that only 35% of a given message's meaning is derived from the actual words we use. These statistics border on the ridiculous, yet it's the reality most of us have to live with.

Learning to be a Skillful Listening Father can open the door to deep understanding and to love, not only for others, but also for ourselves. However, as with any new skill we take on, we must keep a gentle perspective. No matter how hard we try, there will be times when miscommunication simply happens. We can laugh about it and take whatever necessary steps will lead to restored connection and clarity. The very intention of wanting to be a better listener speaks volumes and is often more important to kids than getting it "perfect" every time.

Practice: *Take some time off from practicing to be a Skillful Listening Father and give yourself permission to be "the worst listener in the world!" Relax...enjoy the process of learning.*

26. Develop "second attention at the edge"

Growth and learning takes place in kids in very much the same way that they do in grass and flowers and trees – right at the edges where the old makes room for the new. In flowers, we observe the tiny openings of buds in springtime displaying the first flash of color. In tree leaves and grasses, we can easily see the darker green as it stands in sharp contrast to the new, brighter green out at the edges.

Similarly, we can notice such growing hints and contrasts between the old and the emerging new in our children. We can do that by paying close or "second attention" to those edges where old ways of being and acting are getting ready to fall away, as new areas of expertise and responsibility prepare to burst into bloom. More often than not, the transitions that growth and change require of our kids comes with fear and anxiety attached. If we pay respect – look once again, or pay "second attention" – any time we hear hints of fear or anxiety coming from our kids, we might be curious about the things connected to such concerns. By thinking deeply about creative possibilities in connection with our children's growing edges, we can be of enormous help to them.

Practice: *Pay attention to changes that might be on the verge of unfolding in your children. They are not always readily apparent, as new behaviors often appear virtually overnight. What are you hearing or seeing that tells you they may be on the cusp of change and be feeling anxious? How might you best hold sacred the tender truths they might be needing to share with you?*

Section Two Reflection Questions

What changes have you noticed between you and your kids since you've begun practicing these listening skills?

What conflicts have you been able to resolve since you've been practicing these skills?

What things are you newly curious about or interested in about your kids?

Notes to yourself...

"Listening is a magnetic and strange thing, a creative force….When we are listened to, it creates us, makes us unfold and expand. Ideas actually begin to grow within us and come to life."

~ Brenda Ueland

"What is it you're not saying?"

I had a fascinating experience with a highly balanced masculine and feminine culture two years ago in New Zealand while traveling with a group of women healers. We had been invited to visit a sacred, reservation-like community of the Maori Polynesian culture.

At a gathering of hundreds of men, women and children, I asked the community's medical doctor just what medicine he used for healing many of the illnesses on the island and his reply changed my thinking. He said that they used no medicine whatsoever. None.

If a person was sick in any way, from a cold to cancer, they would call the entire community and all gathered round, including the children. They'd position the ill person in the center and the community would sit. This physician would ask the person one question and one question only: "What is it that you are not saying?" They would all sit and wait for days until this person revealed all of what he or she was keeping to him or herself. The doctor reported a ninety-eight percent healing rate. They were using their own innate wisdom, their own inner guidance and the power of full self-expression, that is, emotional truth, intellectual truth and its interconnect-edness.

~ Dr. Christine Hibbard

27. Learn to let go

In many of the previous practices, I've invited you to attempt to listen without judging, and to tolerate and accept your children much as you find them. I realize those are tall orders. Every father has an ego and a view of the world that makes sense to them. To let go of what we think the world and our children should be like can be a grand challenge. How *do* we let go?

We start by realizing the world is made up of millions of kids who come from different cultures, who are being raised with different parenting styles, and who are experiencing different early life events that are shaping them into who they will one day become. In order to let go of our expectations and "shoulds," we must embrace the reality of diversity. The world does not look any one way. There are few "shoulds." When we let go of thinking the world and its inhabitants should be a certain way, we begin to loosen the need for control. We open ourselves to what exists in reality without the need to force our children to buy into our worldview.

In a sociological study that interviewed a significant number of people at the end of life, three things were mentioned over and over concerning what made for a rich, complete life: living fully, loving well, and … learning to let go. Three important life lessons to model for our children.

Practice: *List a dozen ways that you think your children should be different than they are. Next to that list write down how they actually are. Can you love and appreciate and accept how they are, and let go and listen in ways that* *will allow things to change in directions you might like them to, without the need for force or control?*

28. Listen between the words

Skilled Listening Fathers pay close attention to what children don't say as well as to what they do. They recognize that often kids are monitoring how safe they feel and consequently, what they can reveal. This process often goes on with friends and partners as well. Research has demonstrated that the actual words we use convey less than ten percent of the total information that our kids receive from us. The rest they take from tone, context, body language, and what is *not* said.

Learning to listen for what isn't being said isn't difficult. Body language, stumbling for words, and facial expressions are three things a Listening Father can watch and listen for. As Malcolm Gladwell pointed out in his *New Yorker* article, "The Naked Face," what often isn't being said is readily recognizable simply by looking directly at your child's face. If you suspect something is not being said, ask what will make it safe for your kids to say what they really want to. Then do what is necessary to make it safe for them to speak.

Author and poet, Charles C. Finn said, "I tell you everything that is really nothing, and nothing of what is everything. Do not be fooled by what I'm saying. Please listen carefully and try to hear what I am not saying." Remember, being trustworthy, as I noted earlier, goes a long way in helping children feel safe enough to speak truthfully. And children do want you to hear what it is they are not saying.

Practice: *Over the next few days, observe conversations you have with your children. Ask if there is something that they really want to say, but feel they can't. Ask what you can do to make it safe, so they can tell you what it is they are not saying.*

29. Champion the timid voice

All of us are wiser than any one of us. When two or more kids get together, there are gems of wisdom waiting to be discovered. A timid child though won't offer up these gems for a variety of reasons. Some may feel it is unsafe to speak. Others might not be clear about what it is they want to say.

Making it safe for children to speak freely invites great wisdom out of the mouths of babes. When a Skillful Listening Father champions the timid voice they convey ongoing respect and provide protection from judgments, criticisms, and ridicule in any form. And not just for the timid voices, but for all children all the time. It is from observing such safe treatment that timid voices will cautiously begin speaking up.

Championing the timid voice is much like creating a safe harbor where children can speak truth to power (Skill No. 13). You may feel as though you are not in a position of power over your kids, but it is often difficult for them to speak up nonetheless.

When intimidating or overwhelming elements in any situation are deliberately addressed and removed, respect for those less assertive can make them feel free to speak. More often than not, a timid child will spring to life and introduce a wealth of perspective and insight. A Listening Father actively goes out of his way to solicit ideas and opinions from those children. The resulting ideas and opinions often turn out to be quite surprising to parent and child alike!

Practice: *Identify a child who is normally quiet and reserved in group settings. Next time it's appropriate, see what creative possibilities you can come up with to encourage that child to be more self-expressive.*

30. Listen for inconsistencies

How many times have you had the experience of hearing one of your children speak and their words simply do not ring true? Inconsistencies are mismatches and they frequently occur between what a child says – the content of their communication – and the feeling tone behind the words. Daily exchanges often contain such incongruities. "No problem!" and "I'm not scared" can often mean the exact opposite.

In addition to voice tone, body language can also contradict spoken words. A child proclaiming themselves to be happy while sitting slumped with a frown on their face sends a mixed message. Likewise, a child who laughs nervously as a defense in emotionally loaded circumstances is demonstrating incongruous or inconsistent communication.

A Skillful Listening Father learns to recognize inconsistencies. They listen for the feeling that is expressed even when the words don't match the communication. The feelings communicated through the mixed message will be the more accurate and truthful element in the communication, arising as they do from unconscious, implicit memory. When two feelings seem to be at odds, whatever appears to be appropriate to the situation will be the one to pay close attention to. The trick in addressing inconsistencies, as in much that constitutes skillful listening, is to respond in compassionate ways that do not reinforce or increase defensiveness.

Practice: *Next time you're with a group of kids, listen for mismatches between what a child says and their facial expressions and body postures. Which* do you think is the more authentic communication?

31. Reclaim negative projections

Projection is the well-documented psychological process whereby we unwittingly ascribe our disowned thoughts, feelings and behaviors onto our children or other people. The childhood saying, "It takes one to know one" accurately sums up the mechanism of projection: we see in other people those things that we both like and don't like in ourselves.

What we can't be with, won't let us be. Anytime we find ourselves disproportionately irate at the laziness or selfishness of our children, or at the arrogance of our partner, a close look at these aspects of ourselves is in order. Disproportionate reactions are the "tells" that give us away, that indicate a high probability that we are projecting something we are unwilling to own, out onto other people. Carl Jung called this aspect of us, "the person we would rather not be." These are the parts of ourselves that we have unconsciously disowned or rejected. And we can be pretty confident that with any such parts of ourselves, somewhere along the way, our kids will find a way to reflect those rejected and disowned parts back to us for reclaiming and "owning."

Practice: *Think about three of the most dislikeable qualities in your kids. Take an honest look at yourself and see where those very same qualities might live in you. How might you befriend them in the service of change?*

32. Return to the needs of the present moment

Much of our everyday life is lived in what "recovering neurologist" Robert Scaer calls "the precarious present" moment. Very little of what we talk about with our kids every day deals with in-the-moment current events, needs, or wants. One of the great gifts in being a Skillful Listening Father is a growing ability to serve as a reminder that our lives unfold and take place in the here and now. One way to reclaim the present moment is to inquire about thoughts and feelings as they are occurring. "What does that feel like?" "What do you want right now?" "Is there something you need now that I can help with?" These and other responses help lead the focus back to the present moment. Such responses help us practice mindfulness. And mindfulness helps us be skillful fathers.

The benefit of a present-moment focus is the central theme of Eckhart Tolle's book, *The Power of Now.* In the present moment is where everything that we want and need is rooted, and helping to facilitate that awareness and recognition in and with our children is of inestimable value. Nevertheless, it is not easy to come to fully into the present moment consistently without a lot awareness and practice. And most often what keeps us out of the present moment are fear-based thoughts rooted in negative past experiences.

Practice: *Begin paying close attention to how things feel to you in this moment – in your body and in your mind. Are you thirsty? Hungry? Happy? Sad? Feel a need to get up and move? See how many times in a day you can take a present-moment "break!" Paying attention to such things is actually skillful self-listening, as well as a wonderful model for children to encounter on a regular basis.*

33. Develop methods for skillful self-listening

Skillful Listening Fathers learn to listen deeply to themselves. In their role as a parent, they frequently ask: "What's true for me? What do I want? What can I do to obtain what I want?"

A well-known adage instructs, "If you bring forth what is inside you, it will save you. If you do not bring forth what is inside you, it will destroy you." Listening is the primary way that fathers can discover and cultivate the riches that live deep within themselves.

Another simple and direct way to listen to oneself is to begin a process of discerning one's *ordo amorum* (the order of things we love). Who am I? What do I love? What do I love most? By regularly asking these questions, change happens.

Two all-encompassing self-questions that researchers have found to be enormously powerful when asked over and over again are the very ones at the top of this page: *What's true for me?* and *What do I want?* Fathers who ask these two questions repeatedly will not only help to crystallize wishes, wants, and dreams, but will also help to reinvigorate and re-inspire efforts that may have been temporarily halted due to any number of life's pressing concerns.

Practice: *Spend a month writing a double-entry journal (http://bit.ly/1DEleX3) First, ask and write answers to the two questions above: What's true for me? What do I want? Then come back at the end of a month and write commentary on the entries that you have made the previous month. What common themes emerge? Can you see how this might lead to profound self-listening?*

34. Cultivate patience

Skillful Listening Fathers cultivate patience. Those who have accomplished some measure of proficiency at being patient, share an understanding that hearing children out – helping them get to the heart of the matter – takes time. And it's that time they're willing to spend.

Such fathers possess a ready willingness to *temporarily* suspend whatever needs for self-expression they may have, while they focus on their children without any great need for them to be succinct, speedy or clear in what they have to say. They are not disturbed when a child, who might be struggling with an important subject, rambles or repeats the same thing over and over in different ways. Skillful, patient Listening Fathers carry *Beginner's Ear* (Skill No. 8) with them, letting them frequently hear the same story as if hearing it for the first time.

How exactly does someone go about cultivating patience? First, with practice and a clear understanding of the benefits that patience offers to oneself and others. And by knowing and understanding that children need to tell their stories to a parent who cares, and that there is a freeing, healing value inherent in such telling. These are considerable benefits to offer our children.

Practice: *Experiment with three things that might work to help you be more patient with yourself and your children. Whatever works for you to become more patient is worth discovering and practicing. It is an indicator that you have temporarily put aside your own needs in service to another. Patience is love in action.*

35. Become someone who can hear hard truths

There are many direct ways we let children know we don't want to hear certain things that will upset us. A father might say, "I don't want to hear that," "Let's not go there," or "I don't want to talk about problems, only solutions."

We also have indirect ways we let children know what not to tell us. One way is to simply not be around much. A more common way is for fathers to express anger or frustration in response to things their children say that they don't like. Listening to hard truths forces Listening Fathers to open their hearts and minds to topics that may be emotionally charged. They challenge him to be slow to anger, disagree or criticize (Skill No. 6). But being slow with those reactive responses is exactly what we must do if we want our children to trust us enough to share even their easy truths with us.

What must we do if we truly want to become a father to whom hard truths can be readily told? First of all, we must find *authentic* ways to value, praise and honor such truth-telling. We must also develop increasing capacity to recognize the gifts children bring us, even when their words might initially feel painful and threatening. American artist, James Bishop understood both the power and the difficulty in being able to hear hard truths: "The truth which makes us free is for the most part, the truth which we prefer not to hear."

Practice: *Pay attention when your child stops short of telling you something difficult. Notice what you may be doing to close down the conversation. What might you do to make it safe enough to reopen again?*

36. Express appreciation often and unexpectedly

The research evidence is undeniable: letting our children frequently know that we appreciate them, and the specific things that we appreciate about them, has proven benefits for our own hearts and theirs.

Positive emotions affect the heart and body as much as they do the brain. Dr. Rollin McCraty, a researcher at the Institute of HeartMath, has conducted numerous studies identifying the relationship between emotions and the heart. The heart is in a constant two-way interchange with the brain sending roughly ten times more information to the brain than it receives.

When we experience and express heart-felt emotions like love, care, appreciation and compassion, the heart produces a smooth, rhythmic pattern that looks like gently rolling hills. Appreciation is one of the most concrete and easiest positive emotions for individuals to self-generate and sustain for long periods. Almost anyone can find something to genuinely appreciate in others. By simply recalling a time when you felt sincere appreciation and expressing it, you can increase your heart rhythm coherence, reduce emotional stress and improve your health.

Practice: *If you initially find it difficult to generate feelings of appreciation, start by recalling any past memory that elicits warm feelings. With practice, you will be able to generate feelings of appreciation in real time and no longer need the past time prompting.*

37. Break the "I" habit

Many years ago, before privacy laws were enacted, the New York Telephone Company listened in on phone conversations as part of a research project to discover the most frequently used words in daily conversations. The number one word, they discovered, was "I."

Most of us don't realize how much of our daily talk is about ourselves. It's a habit begun in childhood – one we've never been encouraged to change. Here are a few good reasons to break that habit: the word "I" stifles true dialogue as well as the opportunity to learn anything new about our children as they grow and change. "I" stifles creative parenting, teamwork and discovering new ways to interact with our kids.

When we fathers ask more questions of our kids, and discuss the things on their mind with them using the pronoun "you" (as long as we're not bossing or blaming), a new world begins to open up. Children will be drawn to us and we will win a new level of respect. Skillful Listening Fathers are aware of the benefits of using the word "you" more often than "I."

Practice: *For the next seven days, try to not begin a sentence with "I." Be aware of how many times you refer to yourself in a conversation. As you use the pronoun "I" less and less, notice how people respond to you.*

38. Ask specific, clarifying questions

We often assume we understand what our children mean by the words they use. However, consider this: as mentioned earlier, each of the 800 words that we regularly and repeatedly use in everyday English has an average of 17 different definitions! Other languages have similar limitations. Is it any wonder that we are so frequently surprised to discover that what we thought someone meant, after close questioning, we then discover they meant something else entirely?

A Skillful Listening Father knows that the meanings of words are tricky and subjective. When we engage in dialogue, we frequently speak thoughts off the top of our heads. First thoughts work like first drafts in writing – they require a good editor/listener to clarify meaning and intent. Like a writer attempting to commit a vision to the page, a child may have trouble finding and using words to express all that he or she may be thinking and feeling. By asking specific, clarifying questions a father can frequently help bring a child's subject into clear focus. It's also important to … assume good intent.

How do we know when something needs clarification? One way is to listen for certain words that signal unclear generalizations. Words like "they," "everyone," "always," "never," or "nobody" are a few examples. When ask our kids to clarify or elaborate, such generalizations often end up referring to specific people, places, times and things.

Practice: *Listen for generalizations and globalizations in your next several conversations. They often show up in the words described above. See if you can get a child to become more specific in their speech.*

39. Say what's useful; say what's true

Some fathers can't wait to "get things off their chest" or give their kids "a piece of my mind." They take great pride in "not pulling any punches" and in "telling it like it is." However, this style of communication has a certain kind of unmanaged aggressiveness in it. Skillful Listening Fathers do not respond in this way. Rather, they respond most often with what they know to be factual, true, beneficial and agreeable. They also develop a sense of timeliness – recognizing the "right" or "teachable" moment for saying them.

In other words, out of a sense of genuine affection and care for his kids, a thoughtful and Listening Father realizes that an important element of truth-telling involves under-standing exactly what a child is able and ready to hear. In addition to what is truthful, they consider what will be most useful to their kids. The distinction between the skillful style and the egocentric style is simple and easy to distinguish: one is thoughtful and child-centered, and the other is thoughtless and self-centered, caring little about the real needs and wishes of the child.

How do we best determine what a child might be ready, willing and able to hear? If they are feeling defensive and hurt, they are unlikely to be able to usefully receive "truth-telling." One excellent way to find out what a child is ready to hear and find useful is often … to simply ask them!

Practice: *Think of a situation where you'd like to give "a piece of your mind" to your child. What is your motivation for such action? If you could transform your intention or motivation, how might you speak so that what you have to say could be heard and put to good use?*

Section Three Reflection Questions

What does it feel like when you listen deeply to your children?

What have you heard recently from your kids that you may have found disturbing? How did you respond? If you haven't heard anything, why not?

What have you noticed about your capacity to pay ever closer attention to your children?

Notes to yourself...

"All things, animate and inanimate, have within them, a spirit dimension. They communicate in that dimension to those who can listen."

~ Jerome Bernstein
Jungian Analyst

"Sit down here and tell me about it."

The train clanked and rattled through the suburbs of Tokyo on a drowsy spring afternoon. Our car was comparatively empty – a few housewives with their kids in tow, some old folks going shopping. I gazed absently at the drab houses and dusty hedgerows.

At one station the doors opened, and suddenly the afternoon quiet was shattered by a man bellowing violent, incomprehensible curses. The man staggered into our car. He wore laborer's clothing, and he was big, drunk, and dirty. Screaming, he swung at a woman holding a baby. The blow sent her spinning into the laps of an elderly couple. It was a miracle that the baby was unharmed.

Terrified, the couple jumped up and scrambled toward the other end of the car. The laborer aimed a kick at the retreating back of the old woman but missed as she scuttled to safety. This so enraged the drunk that he grabbed the metal pole in the center of the car and tried to wrench it out of its stanchion. I could see that one of his hands was cut and bleeding. The train lurched ahead, the passengers frozen with fear. I stood up.

I was young then, some twenty years ago, and in pretty good shape. I'd been putting in a solid eight hours of aikido training nearly every day for the past three years. I liked to throw and grapple. I thought I was tough. The trouble was, my martial skill was untested in actual combat. As students of aikido, we were not allowed to fight.

"Aikido," my teacher had said again and again, "is the art of reconciliation. Whoever has the mind to fight has broken his connection with the universe. If you try to dominate people, you are already defeated. We study how to resolve conflict, not how to start it."

I listened to his words. I tried hard. I even went so far as to cross the street to avoid the *chimpira*, the pinball punks who lounged around the train stations. My forbearance exalted me. I felt both tough and holy. In my heart, however, I wanted an absolutely legitimate opportunity whereby I might save the innocent by destroying the guilty.

"This is it!" I said to myself as I got to my feet. "People are in danger. If I don't do something fast, somebody will probably get hurt."

Seeing me stand up, the drunk recognized a chance to focus his rage. "Aha!" he roared. "A foreigner! You need a lesson in Japanese manners!"

I held on lightly to the commuter strap overhead and gave him a slow look of disgust and dismissal. I planned to take this turkey apart, but he had to make the first move. I wanted him mad, so I pursed my lips and blew him an insolent kiss.

"All right!" he hollered. "You're gonna get a lesson in Japanese manners." He gathered himself for a rush at me.

A fraction of a second before he could move, someone shouted "Hey!" It was earsplitting. I remember the strangely joyous, lilting quality of it – as though you and a friend had been searching diligently for something, and he had suddenly stumbled upon it. "Hey!"

I wheeled to my left; the drunk spun to his right. We both stared down at a little, old Japanese man. He must have been well into his seventies, this tiny gentleman, sitting there immaculate in his kimono. He took no notice of me, but beamed delightedly at the laborer, as though he had a most important, most welcome secret to share.

"C'mere," the old man said in an easy vernacular, beckoning to the drunk. "C'mere and talk with me." He waved his hand lightly.

The big man followed, as if on a string. He planted his feet belligerently in front of the old gentleman, and roared above the clacking wheels, "Why the hell should I talk to you?" The drunk now had his back to me. If his elbow moved so much as a millimeter, I'd drop him in his socks.

The old man continued to beam at the laborer. "What'cha been drinkin'?' he asked, his eyes sparkling with interest.

"I been drinkin' sake," the laborer bellowed back, "and it's none of your business!" Flecks of spittle spattered the old man.

"Oh, that's wonderful," the old man said, "absolutely wonderful! You see, I love sake, too. Every night, me and my wife – she's seventy-six, you know – we warm up a little bottle of sake and take it out into the garden, and we sit on an old wooden bench. We watch the sun go down, and we look to see how our persimmon tree is doing. My great-grandfather planted that tree, and we worry about whether it will recover from those ice storms we had last winter. Our tree has done better than I expected, though, especially when you consider the poor quality of the soil. It's gratifying to watch when we take our sake and go out to enjoy the evening - even when it rains!" He looked up at the laborer, eyes twinkling.

As he struggled to follow the old man's conversation, the drunk's face began to soften. His fists slowly unclenched. "Yeah," he said. "I love persimmons, too. . . ." His voice trailed off.

"Yes," said the old man, smiling, "and I'm sure you have a wonderful wife."

"No," replied the laborer. "My wife died." Very gently, swaying with the motion of the train, the big man began to sob. "I don't got no wife. I don't got no home. I don't got no job. I'm so ashamed of myself." Tears rolled down his cheeks; a spasm of despair rippled through his body.

Now it was my turn. Standing there in my well-scrubbed youthful innocence, my make-this-world-safe-for-democracy righteousness, I suddenly felt dirtier than he was.

Then the train arrived at my stop. As the doors opened, I heard the old man cluck sympathetically. "My, my," he said, "That is a difficult predicament, indeed. Sit down here and tell me about it."

I turned my head for one last look. The laborer was sprawled on the seat, his head in the old man's lap. The old man was softly stroking the filthy, matted hair. As the train pulled away, I sat down on a bench. What I had wanted to do with muscle...had been accomplished with love.

~ Terry Dobson

40. Say what you see

Dads: learning to interact with kids in a variety of everyday situations, without making evaluations of any sort, by "saying what you see" clearly, and with few opinions, shows an extremely high level of intelligence and discernment.

When we say what we see, we take our cues from what is present right in front of us. We follow rather than lead. We go where our children are willing and ready to take us. We don't interpret. If a child is frowning, a Skillful Listening Father says, "I see you frowning." It is much more helpful than offering an interpretation, such as: "I see you are angry," or "Why are you sad?"

By saying what we see, we also avoid making comparisons or being judgmental. "I see clothes on the floor" can be a simple statement of observation, without having to carry the judgment: "You are messy."

One central problem with language is that much of it is based on evaluation, interpretation and comparison. As a Listening Father it is a great challenge to find things to say that are *not* interpretations or comparisons. Saying what we see compassionately offers children the opportunity to show and tell us how they see things. It creates the opportunity for us to help our kids go deeper into their experience, and possibly reach "hard truths" they may want and need to share.

Practice: *Look around you. Pick a series of things that you can readily see. Silently say what they are. Notice where judgment tries to enter in. "I see a messy room" is a different statement than the intended neutral assessment,*

"I see clothes on the floor. There are books on the bed. A pair of shoes is on the chair."

41. Use intention clarification

Oftentimes in the heat of high energy discussions with our kids, we may find ourselves at a loss for words. We don't know what to say next. We need some space and a few moments to regroup and gather our thoughts. At these times, it's good for a Skillful Listening Father to have a few "space-making" tools that we can use when necessary.

One such tool is to ask directly what a child's intention is with their communication. They might not immediately know what their intention is, but often, after considering it for awhile, with training many kids will be able to tell you:

"I'm angry and I don't like you right now."

"I'm frustrated trying to talk to you."

"I'm not ready to turn off the computer and go to bed."

Inquiring about a child's intention works remarkably well to get to the heart of many matters. As a child comes up with a clarifying response, a Skillful Listening Father often gains some time to gather his thoughts and offer an appropri-ate response that will further the discussion, rather than close it down or divert it. Such an intervention can serve as a spring-board to even further explorations.

Practice: *Next time you find yourself in an emotionally intense interaction with one of your children, remember to* *pause at some point and simply ask: "What's your intention with what you're saying?" See what kind of response you end up getting in reply.*

42. Maximize the listening environment

The places where we listen to our kids can affect the experience either negatively or positively. There are many places where speaking and listening to children is actually inappropriate and would adversely affect an interaction. Some obvious examples would be trying to have a conversation during a movie, in a library, at a music recital, sporting event, or during a memorial service or a wedding.

Distractions also diminish the listening experience. For example, interruptions from cell phones or other attention distracters like TVs and radios can impede the listening experience. Skilled Listening Fathers avoid unnecessary distractions.

They also maximize the listening environment when they are clear about the purpose of important conversations and the time limits available for them. Maximizing the listen-ing environment is so important that a Skilled Listening Father will put off a discussion that cannot be held in a place where listening can ideally flourish until he is in a place where it actually can.

Practice: *Identify half a dozen things that you can think of that go into making up an ideal listening environment for you in your role as a father. They might include things like time of day (some children and parents listen better in the morning; others in the afternoon or evening), physical*

*space, indoors or out, time constraints and distractions
you can avoid (for example, turn off your cell phone), etc.*

43. Learn to listen to your own lacunae

The ways we are raised and the experiences we
have as children significantly shape how we see the world
and behave as fathers. Our brains learn early to pay
attention to certain things – especially threats to our well-
being – and filter out others. The result is that spaces or
gaps form in our knowledge and perceptions. Known as
lacunae in the medical literature, these spaces in our
neurological network operate as a kind of filtering system
influencing seeing, listening, or speaking. Some things
that work as powerful filters are painful child-hood
memories, strong family beliefs, unexamined assumptions, personal prejudices, and unconscious expectations.

Many fathers operate with awareness of these
filters only when some glaring omission, error or oversight
makes them so obvious that they can no longer be denied.
For example, a belief that kids who say "No" to their
parents are insolent and disrespectful will stand in stark
relief to the research that shows how important learning to
say "No" is for high self-esteem and emotional
intelligence.

The first thing for a Skillful Listening Father to do
about their lacunae or filters is to recognize that they exist
in each of us. Dispelling ignorance of them allows us to be
curious and provides the possibility for exploration and
examination. This self-awareness then allows us to be
more open and compassionate with our children's and our

own shortcomings.

Practice: *Based upon things that you find yourself forget-ting or repeatedly overlooking, begin to notice what some of your own psychological "holes" as a father might be.*

44. Practice Strategic Questioning

Strategic questions have a number of elements that make them unique and set them apart from run-of-the-mill, everyday questions. Developed by San Francisco-based activist Fran Peavey, Strategic Questions are asked with the intention to reveal ambiguity and open up fresh options for explorations with our kids. They can often be tough questions because they break through the façade of false confidence and reveal the profound uncertainty that underlies all reality. Nevertheless, they invite movement toward growth and new possibilities. Strategic Questions empower us as well as our children to create strategies for change in all areas of life.

There are eight key features that distinguish a Strategic Question. First a Strategic Question is a helpful, dynamic challenge that encourages movement and change. Instead of "where should I apply to college?" a Strategic Question might ask, "What area and with which professors

A Strategic Question encourages options. Instead of "Who might we get to help us?" a more dynamic possibility might be, "Which parents can we support and ally with to help build co-operative parenting synergies?"

A third feature of Strategic Questions is that they are empowering. Examples often begin with the query, "What would it take …?" For example, "What would it take to make you feel your role as a Skillful Listening Father had ever-expanding purpose and meaning?"

Two more features of Strategic Questions are that they don't ask "Why?" and they cannot be answered "Yes" or "No." Questions that ask "Why?" close down creative options and often generate guilt and defensiveness. Questions that can be answered "Yes" or "No" often only skim the surface or bring dialogue and inquiry to a dead end.

Next, Strategic Questions address taboo topics. There is tremendous power to foster change and growth inherent in them, because they challenge our underlying values and assumptions. An example of such a question might be "What was it that kept us from talking about our grandmother's cancer before she died?"

A seventh aspect of Strategic Questions is that they tend to be simply structured, focusing on one thing at a time. "What one thing can you do to make your homework more enjoyable?" or "What can we do to patch things up between us?"

Finally, Strategic Questions assume essential equality. They are deeply respectful of children and their capacity to change and grow in healthy ways. They are positive, life-affirming inquiries designed and intended to support organic growth and change in our children … and in ourselves.

Practice: *Spend a week asking your kids Strategic Questions based on the eight characteristics. See how much depth comes out of the questions. For deepening your understanding of yourself, and your role as a Listening Father, write 25 Strategic Questions about that* *role and see if you can live your way into the answers. Be forewarned, your role as a father may be changed in unexpected and profound ways!*

45. The ears can be ready when the heart's just not

Every father has discussion topics that generate some concern and anxiety. In his book, *The Magical Child*, Joseph Pearce recognized: "Anxiety is the enemy of intelligence," and those things that we fathers can't face or speak about directly, have great power over our lives whether we're aware of it or not. These taboo topics are often guilt or shame-based – some unfortunate incident from our past that lives buried in the depths of our psyche. Nevertheless, they live in us like bear traps or live wires, and anytime such topics are raised, they set off a great charge of strong emotion. We often end up being emotionally triggered – irrationally reactive – and many fathers find the experience painful and surprising to both themselves and to their kids.

As with much that has to do with skillful listening, the first step in dealing with taboo topics is to become aware that talking about menstruation, for example, often makes men uncomfortable. Money, success, sex, loss and death head up many father's lists. But the specific topics are really second-ary. What's primary for a Skillful Listening Father to know is that a pre-existing uneasiness is triggered by such topics, and that children who present them for discussion are most likely not trying to deliberately upset us. Taboo topics can be a critical stumbling block to hearing other hard truths.

Practice: *Over the next week, find a topic that feels taboo or unsettling and invite your children to talk about it. Death, love, sex, and money are good trigger topics. Notice how it feels when the ears are ready to hear but the heart is not. How can you hold your heart open to fully hear what your children want to say?*

46. Don't blame the victim

It is all too common in many cultures to place responsibility for violations of respect and dignity on people who have suffered. We blame the victim. It is human to feel that the victims are responsible in some way – it puts such problems "out there," and helps protect us from anxiety about becoming victims ourselves.

Generally, blaming the victim makes us feel more powerful and more in control of our lives. Clearly, we reason, we are smarter, stronger, healthier, luckier, and have our lives more together, so nothing like that could ever happen to us.

Listening to our children's "victim stories" takes practice and skill. It's important to do and easy to inadvertently and unwittingly slip into a blaming-the-victim stance. Childhood often presents serious suffering with it and kids often need to tell their story over and over to a willing listener. A Skillful Listening Father listens with fresh ears as often as possible, curious and open to the possibility that some sort of resolution underlies such expression and is longing to happen.

Practice: *The next time one of your children raises a difficult experience that they may have already told you about, be willing to hear it again, to listen deeply with open ears, mind and heart. See if you can hear something new, all the while trusting that being listened to listening is often an important part of healing.*

47. Recognize your own "exit strategies"

In addition to "anxiety being the enemy of intelligence," it also drives many of our "exit strategies." Exit strategies are the things we fathers use to turn away from situations that make us anxious. Anxiety and exit strategies, if not skillfully attended to, work against skillful listening.

Exit strategies can take almost any form: daydreaming, pill-popping, drinking coffee or alcohol, overworking, eating sweets, smoking – the list is endless. Brain scientist, Robert Scaer calls them impediments to the "precarious present" moment. Anything that we move towards in an attempt to eradicate or reduce anxiety can serve as an exit strategy.

Learning to identify, recognize and respond positively to exit strategies can serve several purposes. First of all, it helps us to recognize when we're feeling anxious. Many of us fathers rarely know – we turn towards our exit strategies before we are ever consciously aware of our anxiety. A skilled listener learns about their exit strategies and learns to recognize and address the anxiety or fear that creates them.

A primary reason to pay attention to exit strategies is that we can begin to learn new ways to deal with our stress and anxiety. Instead of going off to grab a beer, we can consid-er hanging in, exploring what's true for us, and asking for what we want instead. We can begin to skillfully listen to ourselves as we listen more skillfully to our children.

Practice: *Pay close attention the next time you feel anxious. Be curious about what anxiety feels like in your mind and body. Is it a tension in your stomach or lower back? A constriction in your chest or throat? A pain in your neck? By learning to recognize anxiety's telltale sensations in our body, we can then take steps to address it directly.*

48. Practice the power of attunement

Attunement is one of the most powerful forces on the planet. It begins as resonance in the mother's womb when the baby attunes to the mother's voice. It continues throughout life in our intimate relationships or with colleagues or friends and our children – the feeling of being "at one" with them.

Attunement is not the same as agreement. A father can be attuned to a child and respectfully disagree, while continuing to guide and parent them. With skillful listening, fathers can listen, withhold judgment and take in what children say, but not necessarily agree. Our bodies recognize when we are in attunement and it feels good!

From recent neuroscience research, we know that attunement also feels good in the brain. A brain under stress becomes disorganized and attunement helps soothe and organize it – a true soothing of the savage beast. ☺

Practice: *When you listen to your children, imagine yourself as an instrument in an orchestra. Allow them to play the notes they must play and do not judge or try to change the music. Allow your own music to play, with the intention of joining them to rock and roll together.*

49. Practice taking crap

In *Seeking Enlightenment Hat By Hat*, novelist Nevada Barr writes about working in law enforcement. One day a grizzled old veteran let her in on a little secret: the real job of a peace officer is to "take crap." However, he neglected to offer her many skillful ways to actually go about doing that.

When children send us negative, "stinky" messages – anger, criticism, or complaints – it can sometimes feel as if they are hurling pointed barbs in our direction. One tip: never stay seated or standing directly in front of such expressions. In order to continue skillfully listening without suffering harm, stand up, walk back and forth in front of the child, or stand or walk alongside. Keep yourself out of the direct line of their communication. A moving target is much harder to hit.

For the most part, children in such a state will not even notice, and moving serves as a disciplined way to fill in the gap between hearing and reacting over-emotionally in return. This is contrary to the way fathers have been taught to deal with disturbing people and situations. Mostly we're taught to simply sit and ignore it, or to throw the "crap" right back. But moving or "dancing" with a disturbing situation, rather than simply "taking it," is an extremely useful and worthwhile personal practice.

Practice: *Next time you're in an emotionally charged exchange with your kids, remember to get up and move. Stand and pace or walk side by side in close proximity. See how it affects what you hear the speaker saying and your ability to be non-reactive with them.*

50. Learn to say "No" with ruthless compassion

Saying "No" skillfully can be challenging for fathers. It can be a challenge to set firm limits. But when we don't set and hold such limits without rancor, we can end up feeling weak and resentful. A simple and direct "No, I am not able to listen to you right now" is one simple solution.

When children request our attention, it's fair to take time to think it over. We can do so and get back to them later. Do we have the time to really listen? If not, then "No" is the honest answer. We can use an empathic "No" if we find ourselves listening to things that are attacking or harmful. It is not until we can actually say "No," that our "Yes" means "Yes" and our "No" really comes to mean "No".

Here are five different ways to say "No." 1. The direct "No": "No" means "No"; 2. The reflecting "No": we acknowledge the content and feeling of the child's request, then add the assertive refusal at the end; 3. The reasoned "No": we give a brief and genuine reason for the refusal without opening up further negotiation; 4. The rain check "No": A way of saying "No" to a specific request without giving a definite "No"; 5. The broken record: Repeat the simple statement of refusal again and again. No explanation, just repeat it. It's often necessary to use this with persistent requests, especially from persistent children.

Practice: *Pay attention to times when you say "Yes" and later wish you had said "No." Find a way to go back and offer a "retroactive No." In other words, just because we've said "Yes" initially, doesn't mean we can't say "No" later, and say "No" the next time if feels right to do so. Becoming a Skillful Listening Father does not mean we have to listen to everyone and everything all the time.*

51. Watch for compassion fatigue

The world is filled with pain and suffering. Families are dangerous places where few members get through life without some heartache or traumatic experiences. Some-times, listening to the pain and suffering of others, especially our children, can cause us to close off emotionally.

What does a father do when there is so much suffering in the world and it is painful to feel so vulnerable? How does a father listen to the "full catastrophe," to use Zorba's term, and not fall victim to compassion fatigue? Make it a point to see the good that is as equally abundant in your life as much as the pain and suffering. That's one thing. Practicing gratitude is another one. It's one of the best ways to remain open and ready to reach out to listen and be able to give and receive from others. For it's not so much the ears we use to hear, as it is our hearts.

Practice: *Find the gift, the abundance in the world around you this very minute. Look at the clouds, the sun, or the rain outside your window. Remember that you are part of a creation beyond all comprehension. Breathe in a belly full of that mystery and grace.*

52. Create a community of practice

We like doing things together with people who like doing things with us. When a group of Listening Fathers come together and agree to meet and support each other's growing and learning, extraordinary possibilities begin to emerge.

Learning and practice are infinitely more fun and results are more easily accomplished when we fathers do it with others, when we organize what's known as a "community of practice." Ask friends, colleagues or members of your spiritual community to practice with you. Small, faith-based groups have been quite effective in helping fathers learn to listen skillfully.

As we fathers work with others learning to be skilled listeners, great understanding for the difficult and unending details of the work result. There is an understanding of the struggles required to meet the challenges of becoming a Skillful Listening Father in a world that mostly celebrates talkers. An expanding community of Listening Fathers practicing together has the potential to powerfully transform the lives of our children.

Practice: *Ask a few of your father friends or colleagues to buy this book and create a "Listening Club" dedicated to helping each other learn to become skillful Listening Fathers. You can meet every week for a year and discuss and practice one skill at a time, or create your own timeline. Spiritual groups have found working collectively with this book helps them live the Golden Rule on a daily basis. See what your group discovers and write to me about your experiences. I'd love to listen to you.*

Section Four Reflection Questions

Which areas of your relationships with your children have been positively transformed by practicing the skills in this book?

Who do I think would benefit from receiving a copy of this book?

Who can you ask to join you in a Community of Practice in learning to be a more Skillful Listening Father?

Notes to yourself...

The Early Life Events Impact History

Mark Brady, Ph.D. and Jennifer Austin Leigh, Psy.D.

Instructions:

1. Place a check mark next to any phrase that describes an event that happened at any time in your life.

2. Place the letter "R" next to any phrase that describes an event that occurred more than once in your life (Repeated).

3. Place the letter "S" next to any phrase that describes an event that happened that caused you to feel over-whelmed, helpless, terrified, rage-filled or frozen (Shock).

Harm by commission
(Direct hurts others):

Physical, sexual verbal or emotional abuse

Disrespectful treatment (e.g. insults, lies)

Punitive discipline

Valued for achievements – not who you are

Unreasonably high adult expectations

Ignoring or rejecting of painful emotions

Love or attention conditional on your good behavior

Racism, sexism

Over-control by caretakers

Harm by omission
(Unmet needs):

Physical or emotional neglect

Insufficient nurturing contact, holding or nonsexual touch

Lack of opportunities to form attachments

Lack of stimulation

Lack of autonomy

Unfulfilled promises

Lack of communication

Left out of school activities

Important events unacknowledged

Situational harm (Caused by life circumstances; indirect):

Prenatal or birth trauma

Illnesses, injuries, medical procedures or surgeries

Subjected to general anesthesia or IV sedation

Loss of attachments (separation or death)

Short separation (depends on age)

Over-stimulation

Developmental frustrations and fears

Inescapable restraints

Major changes (e.g. new sibling, home, or school)

Primary caretaker dysfunction (e.g. anxiety, grief, anger, illness)

Primary caretaker disputes, separation or divorce

Primary caretaker alcoholism or drug abuse

Dysfunctional nuclear or extended family system

Natural disasters (e.g. fires, floods, earthquakes, tornadoes, hurricanes)

Exposure to violence (through real life or the media)

Other frightening events

Disappointments or unforeseen occurrences

Arguments with caretakers, peers or siblings

Scoring:

If you indicated more than two or three items with an "R" or an "S" there is a high probability that you have been exposed to repeated or one-time shock trauma experiences. These experiences very likely have had a significant impact on your life in the past and may continue to impact your life today. Such experiences are theorized to live in the brain as physically encapsulated groups of neurons, and in the body as residual "energy cysts." They interfere with our ability to listen skillfully to another as they distort our version of reality and close our heart to a great deal of love and acceptance. We untangle the present by unraveling the knots of the past, and so being listened to with care and compassion is a first step in beginning to clear the body of these residual experiences. On the following page is a list of resources from recent neuropsychology and traumatology research that the astute reader is encouraged to investigate further.

Adapted from:
Tears and Tantrums by Aletha J. Solter, Shining Star Press, 1998

Healing Resources ~~

David Baldwin's Trauma Information Center
http://www.trauma-pages.com

Peter Levine's Foundation for Human Enrichment
http://www.traumahealing.com

Bessel van der Kolk's Boston Trauma Center
http://www.traumacenter.org

Ron Kurtz's Hakomi Institute
http://www.hakomiinstitute.com/main.htm

Francine Shapiro's EMDR Institute
http://www.emdr.com/shapiro.htm

Pat Ogden's Sensorimotor Psychotherapy Institute
http://sensorimotorpsychotherapy.org/faculty.html

Damasio, Antonio (1999). *The Feeling of What Happens: Body and Emotion in the Making of Consciousness.* NY: Harcourt Brace & Company

Luskin, Frederic (2001). *Forgive for Good: A Proven Prescription for Health and Happiness.* SF: Harper

Rothchild, Babette (2000). *The Body Remembers: The Psychophysiology of Trauma and Trauma Treatment* NY: WW Norton

Siegel, Dan (1999). *The Developing Mind: Toward a Neurobiology of Interpersonal Experience* NY: Guilford Press

Conclusion

The power of practice

Transforming into a Skilled Listening Father can be an emotionally and spiritually challenging endeavor. Many feelings and new realizations arise as we attempt to learn about our children and ourselves. Nevertheless, it is a challenge well worth turning toward. The ongoing practice of listening transforms not only our children with its healing attention and compassionate focus, but it transforms fathers as well. With practice, we come to have more compassion, wisdom and solutions for helping children successfully navigate life.

Skilled Listening Fathers lead lives that are more peaceful and successful. There is no other skill on the planet that has the power to positively change so many people with so little investment of time and energy – the time put into practice. As David Augsburger so eloquently told us in the beginning of this book: "Listening is so close to being loved that most people don't know the difference." In practicing how to skillfully listen, fathers model the possibility of spreading more love and peace throughout a world that sorely needs it. The power is in the practice.

The power of attunement

Attunement is one of the most powerful forces on earth. It starts in the mother's womb and ideally continues all through life. Unfortunately attunement occurs less often than is ideal, as people simply do not know how best to attune to others. Skillful listening is an extraordinary way to move into attunement. You can practice and learn what it sounds like and what it feels like in the mind and body. Attunement heals.

The power of creating a listening culture

Creating a global community of Skillful Listening Fathers – to teach and model for children how to use listening as a basis to connect in ways that benefit everyone. We know from recent research that positive interpersonal connections grow body, mind and soul. Groups of people working together at becoming Skillful Listening Fathers create a more mindful, peaceful, understanding, creative, cooperative world. I invite you to join together with me in this mission.

A Listening Manifesto

I believe I have the power and potential to change my life and create more love and peace in the world.

I believe listening is one key to attuning with others to create magnificent relationships at home, work, church, temple, and play.

I believe listening is a learnable and teachable skill.

I believe that others can learn to listen and attune.

I believe others want to speak and be deeply heard, and they want to learn to deeply listen.

I believe I have an open heart that will grow only larger and more open as I learn to listen.

I believe the most abundant harvests in my relationships are yet to come as I learn to listen.

I believe as I change my life through listening I will be rewarded in my relationships and work.

I believe by using my listening skills I will be more fulfilled, happier and successful in life.

I believe that working with others to learn skillful listening is of enormous help.

I believe my ultimate gift to my family, community and the world at large, is the legacy of listening and all the transformative power it holds. I am dedicated to transforming myself and others, and leaving the world a better, richer place for me having lived and listened in it.

116

Listening Skills Bibliography for Fathers

Brady, Mark (2015). *Noble Listening.* Langley, WA: Paideia Press.

Brady, Mark (Ed.) (2003). *The Wisdom of Listening.* Somerville, MA: Wisdom Publications.

Burley-Allen, Madelyn (1995). *Listening : The Forgotten Skill (A Self-Teaching Guide).* NY: John Wiley.

Lindahl, Kay (2003). *Practicing the Sacred Art of Listening.* Woodstock, VT: Skylight Paths.

Nichols, Michael P. (1995). *The Lost Art of Listening.* New York: The Guilford Press.

Patterson, K., Grenny, J., McMillan, R. & Switzler, A. (2002). *Crucial Conversations.* NY: McGraw-Hill.

Rosenberg, Marshall B. (2003). *Nonviolent Communication: a Language of Life.* Encinitas, CA: Puddledancer.

Shafir, Rebecca Z. (2000). *The Zen of Listening: Mindful Communication in the Age of Distraction.* Wheaton, IL: Quest Books.

Steil, Lyman and Bommelje, Rick (2004*). Listening Leaders.* Edina, MN: Beaver's Pond Press, Inc.

About the Author:

Mark Brady is an award-winning author, parent educator, and trainer. He has taught graduate courses in skillful listening for the last dozen years. He has edited the listening anthology, **The Wisdom of Listening** and written numerous articles for journals and national magazines. He is the prize-winning author of a number of books. Two most recent are **entitled *Noble Listening* and *How Parents Screw Us Up (without really meaning to)*.** They can be ordered from bookstores or on the Internet or by emailing: paideia@gmail.com. His most popular book- ***Safe and Secure: A Guide to Parenting with the Brain in Mind*** - will be re-released in 2015.

Contact Us

We hope you enjoyed this book and the transformations taking place in your life as you've practiced some of the skills. We invite you to send us your comments, ideas and any stories you'd like to share at the addresses below. We'd be delighted to hear from you!

To contact Mark Brady for more information:
Email: committedparent@gmail.com
P.O. Box 1294
Langley, WA
Office: (206) 201-2212

To Order:

To order copies of *A Father's Book of Listening*
Send a check for $14.95 (includes shipping and handling) to: Paideia Press, P.O. Box 1294, Langley, WA 98260 (Includes tax and shipping.)

Please remember to include your shipping information. Orders of 20 or more are discounted. Please contact us for pricing and shipping information.

For your convenience, *A Father's Book of Listening* may also be purchased digitally or in print at Amazon.com or through your local bookseller.

Made in the USA
Lexington, KY
19 April 2017